This book belongs to:

Lupita

D1378254

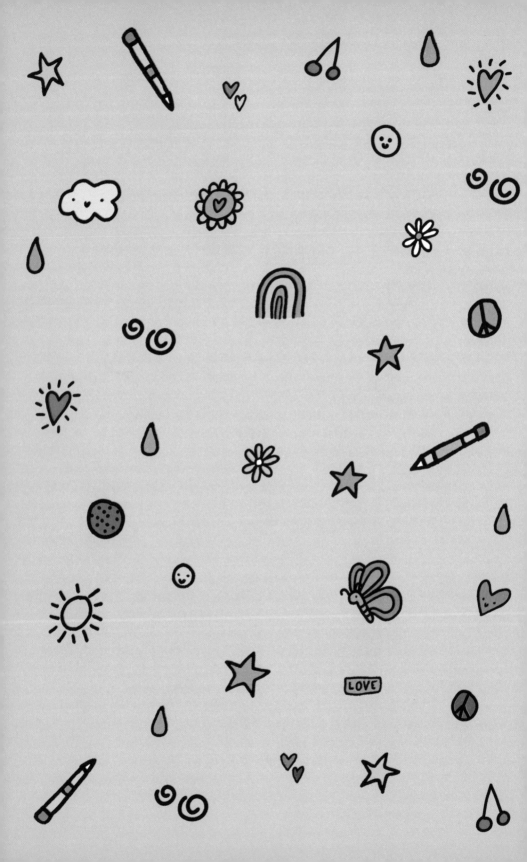

Find Your Rainbow

Jenipher Lyn

Crown
New York

Dear Friend,

Can I just tell you how AWESOME you are?!

Life will throw some curveballs at you, from school grades to challenging friendships, but don't lose hope! Follow your heart and go after your dreams! I hope this book helps you find your happy path, your rainbow.

You will find your rainbow when you are true to yourself and learn what you care about most. Life is far from perfect, and sometimes we're thrown off course, but following your rainbow will help you stay afloat.

Use this book to tell your story. These are your pages. Design and decorate them any way you'd like! Use stickers (yay, stickers!), collage, and color, and by the time you finish, you'll know what your rainbow is!

Much Love!

Jenipher Lyn

Contents

Draw a self-portrait

when you start this book.

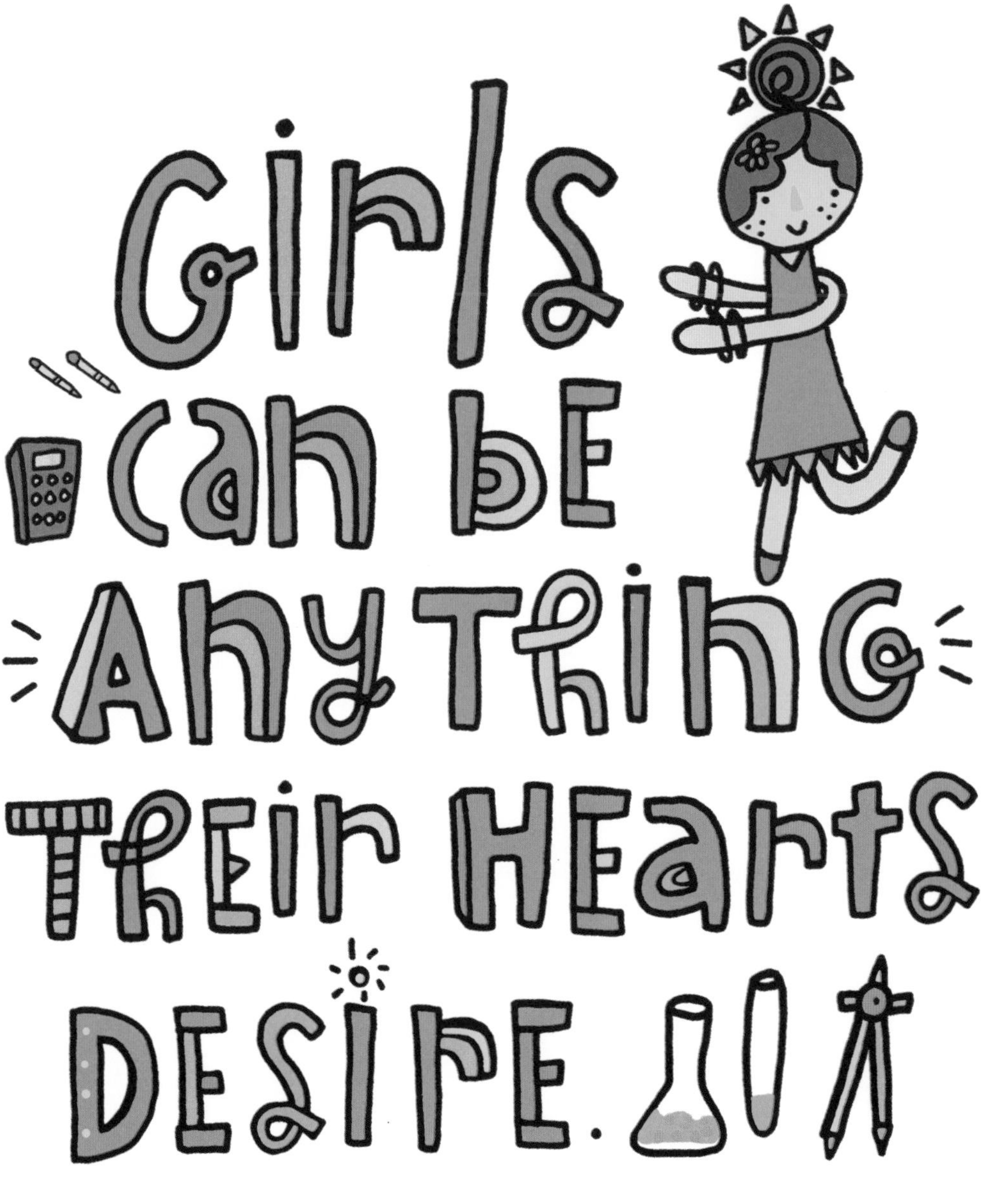
Girls can be anything their hearts desire.

Chapter One

Believe in yourself

You are AWESOME.
Just the way you are. Seriously!

The first step to believing in yourself is figuring out who you really are (instead of the person everyone else wants you to be).

Your true self is the part of you that dances when you think no one is looking. It lets you sing at the top of your lungs even though you might be a little tone-deaf.

List things that
disguise
your true self.

List things that
reveal
your true self.

Be true to YOU

It's hard not to compare yourself to people you know. Their lives may seem perfect, and they may act like everything is great. The truth is that the most popular, smartest, richest, and prettiest people still have problems.

It can be upsetting to feel like you don't measure up. Just remember, you're not alone.

Fill in the thought bubbles below with questions that can help free the real you. (I've added a couple to get you started.)

Are these my real friends?

I <3 to draw. Why don't I do it more?

Design Your Dream Wardrobe

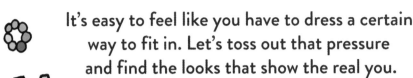

It's easy to feel like you have to dress a certain way to fit in. Let's toss out that pressure and find the looks that show the real you.

Draw your favorite outfit, the one that makes you feel awesome. Then draw your dream outfit!

Favorite
Outfit

Dream
Outfit

Do you ever feel like you keep all your emotions bottled up?

Decorate labels for the feelings you keep bottled up in these closed jars.

It feels so much better to share your feelings with the world, to help rid yourself of negative emotions.

Label your feelings as they escape from these open jars.

Circle all the words that sound like you.

Musician

Messy

Sad

Good friend

Lonely

Homebody

Book lover

Writer

Artistic

Helpful

Animal lover

Anxious

Serious

Giver

Quiet

Happy

Athletic

Movie lover

Sports lover

Proud

Chatty

Dancer

Friendly

Boy crazy

Silly

Smart

Organized

Family oriented

Award Yourself!

I believe in you. And you should, too! Draw a ribbon for believing in yourself and for anything you've done that wasn't easy for you.

Tried something NEW!

Helped
_____

Walked my dog!

Life is too short to put yourself in a mold.

Believing in your dreams starts with you.

But you don't have to do it all alone. Go find someone (a friend, family member, or teacher) who embraces the real you—good traits and bad—and wants to help you shine. This is especially important for the days you don't believe in yourself.

Don't let anyone discourage you from your dreams—not even the insecure person who lives inside you.

write your

COOLest

Dream jobs

here.

- cat vet in space

YOU'VE GOT THIS!

My great-aunt Kiki's house was my safe place. She was the person I went to when I needed a trusted friend, a listening ear, and a comforting meal. She made me feel heard and loved, and she was always calm and understanding. Someone like this, even just one person, makes ALL the difference in the world.

WhO BELIEVES IN you?

Sometimes in movies and books, people who started off as frenemies end up friends. I've listed a few below in one column. In the other, try to add some more from YOUR favorite books and movies!

Jen's List	My List
Judy Hopps + Nick Wilde Zootopia	
Han Solo + Princess Leia Star Wars	
Moana + Maui Moana	
Joy + Sadness Inside Out	

Relationships take time

Even if someone isn't your go-to person right now, that doesn't mean they won't be in the future—or that you won't meet someone new. Give others a chance to believe in you by showing them who you really are.

Who do you want to get to know better?

1.

2.

3.

4.

If you had a weird superpower,* what would it be? Draw it, too!

* I would create a herd of magic sheep to protect me! (And then cuddle them all.)

Chapter Two

A FRIEND GIVES YOU the FREEDOM to BE YOU

Friends. Or No Friends . . . Yet.

What makes someone a good friend?

★ Someone you can talk to

★ Someone you can count on

★ Someone who understands you

Maybe you don't need an enormous group of friends,
just one or two people who really "get" you.
And you don't always have to see one another
in person to be there for each other.

Some friendships will be strong for years,
and some will last a little while.
But they all shape who you are.

Draw some Friendship Bracelets!

*draw nail polish, too!

November 19

Dear Diary,

A new girl moved into the neighborhood. She's my age and started playing with my best friend. I saw them playing on the swings yesterday and felt sad because they didn't invite me to join them. What if the new girl ends up stealing my best friend from me? Then who will be my best friend?

November 29

Dear Diary,

It's okay now! We're all friends! We played freeze tag yesterday and it was really fun. Now I have two best friends! :)

Design emojis that are perfect for you and your friends.

Now text Someone with your new emojis.

Design the case, too!

27

Friendship isn't always easy.

Sometimes you don't get along or agree on everything, but true friends are there to support each other, no matter what.

what if you have friends and still feel lonely?

Try your best to stay positive and remember that you won't always feel this way. In the meantime, you can seek out a new friend who shares your interests, values, and sense of humor. Clubs and after-school activities are a great way to meet new friends. Is there a club at school that interests you?

Putting the Social in Social Media

Even though social media can sometimes make you feel left out, there are positive aspects to it, too!

It keeps you connected, even when you can't be together—especially when you or a friend moves away and you aren't able to see each other all the time.

There are also a lot of safe ways to meet friends with the same interests as you on social media.

Do you love animals? Love to cook? Want to help the environment? There are many resources online for you to explore! Just make sure you ask a parent or guardian before you meet up with a new friend or join an organization that you found online.

Three's a Crowd

Bff 4eva

Hanging out in a trio can be especially difficult because it sometimes feels like one of you is being left out. And unfortunately, social media can highlight it when your best friends are doing something amazing without you.

It's important to remember that these situations are not always intentional, and you should try to make sure that you're not doing the same thing to others accidentally. Take silly selfies together instead of focusing on the moments you missed.

Write a message to a friend who may be feeling left out.

DESSERT ISLAND

If you were stranded on a delicious dessert island, who would you want to be there with and what type of dessert would it be made of? Draw you and your friend on your special sweet island below!

Where the Friends Are

Finding the right friends can take time. Sometimes it's easier to meet friends who like the same things you do. If you like to draw or be creative, try joining an art class. If you're a competitive person or you like being active, try a chess club or a sports team.

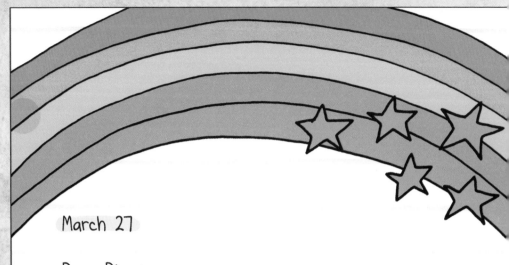

March 27

Dear Diary,

I don't have very many friends, and the ones I do have tease me. All the mean things they say, like making fun of how frizzy my hair is or how babyish my shoes with cartoon characters are, make me feel really bad about myself. I don't want to hang out with them anymore, but I don't have any other friends. :(

fren·e·my
plural noun: frenemies
A person who pretends to be your friend but really dislikes you.

Frenemies may make you feel like you have to hide your true self to fit in.

Have you ever done "Operation: Make My Room Cooler" before having friends over?

Step 1: Hide posters of cute celebrities behind calendars.

Step 2: Move favorite music and movies to the closet.

Step 3: Clean up stuffed animals. (Put behind the pillows?)

Step 4: Hide diary! (Underwear drawer, perhaps?)

It can take so much energy trying to hide things you love.

Sometimes it's easier to be alone than to be with people who don't let you be yourself.

Pretending to NOT like something is SO DRAINING.

You've got the power!

If someone is not treating you nicely, you can choose not to be their friend. You may have to hang out with people if they are part of your friend group, but try your best to be kind to them—and yourself.

Yes	No	
☐	☐	Do I feel comfortable when we're together?
☐	☐	Does she make me laugh?
☐	☐	Do we have a good time together?
☐	☐	Do we have similar interests?
☐	☐	Do we have fun just being silly?

Gut Check

Sometimes a friend may push you to do something you think is wrong. Always listen to your inner voice for guidance. If you're still not sure what to do, here are some questions you can ask yourself:

Does it make me nervous?
Would my parents allow it?
Could I get in trouble?
Is there a chance someone could get hurt?
Could something terrible happen?

Listen to your little voice and don't forget that even friends can do the wrong thing sometimes.

What's Your Excuse?

Have you ever been invited somewhere you didn't want
to go (or with people you didn't feel comfortable around)?

My mom taught me to use her as an excuse to get out of tough
situations by saying, "Oh no! My mom said I can't go!" But if
you end up somewhere that makes you uncomfortable, just say
you have a stomachache and call a parent to take you home.

Below are some difficult questions a friend may ask you.
Write down the excuse you'd use to get out of each situation.

When my friend says . . .

I say . . .

You don't know her,
but do you want to sleep
over at my friend's house?

Do you want to have a
boy-girl party?

I dare you to steal her
backpack.

Do you want to sneak out
tonight?

I dare you to send an
embarrassing photo to
your crush.

Do you want to sneak
into an R-rated movie?

I give you Permission to say NO... then eat a cookie to REWARD yourself!

What cheers you up when you're having a terrible day?

Books	Songs	Movies
1.	1.	1.
2.	2.	2.
3.	3.	3.
4.	4.	4.

TV Shows	Games	Other
1.	1.	1.
2.	2.	2.
3.	3.	3.
4.	4.	4.

Have you seen someone get picked on?

Did you stick up for them? Walk away? Wish you had the courage to save them? It may be hard, but always try to stand up for what is right. If you are uncomfortable with how someone is being treated, tell an adult immediately. You can also try to comfort the person who is getting bullied and make a new friend!

Bully-Free Zone

Are YOU being bullied?

First, find someone you trust to talk to. There is
NOTHING wrong with asking for help. Sometimes
it might be too scary to tell someone what is
happening to you.

If you are too nervous, try writing a note
to an adult you trust.

Imagine having a safe conversation with a bully.
What would you say to them about how
their actions make you feel?

Try writing a practice note here.

Stick up For each other
(and yourself).
BE Brave!

Everyone has crushes.

We often have crushes on people who are out of reach, like celebrities. But sometimes you may start crushing on a friend. If they are meant to be more than your friend, it will happen because of who you really are and what you have in common, so just be yourself.

And try not to let your crush take up so much space in your brain that it crowds out all the other great things going on in that awesome life of yours.

Decorate a notebook with a design about your crush!

Chapter Three

It will! I promise!

Life can be hard sometimes, no matter what age you are.

A friend might have hurt your feelings. You might have missed a goal at your soccer game, or maybe you received a low grade on a project. Hard times can also happen when there are big changes in your life that are out of your control.

It's okay to feel a little sad or upset when this happens. But talking to a friend, getting a big hug, or taking time to rest might make you feel better.

Even a bad day can be made better.
Try one of these ideas to help
change your mood.

Write your feelings down in a diary.

Listen to music.

Read a book.

Binge-watch your favorite TV show.

Watch a funny movie.

Do some yoga, play a sport, or
do something else physical.

Dance to some music.

Hug your pet.

Draw, knit, or create something.

Paint your nails.

Talk to a friend or family member.

Help someone with their problem.

Milk + cookies = YAY!

As you get older, big changes start happening to your body, and you start feeling things a LOT more! You might feel moody, sad, or anxious—and then happy and silly—all within a short period of time. When it seems like you're riding a giant roller coaster of emotions, capture some of your feelings in the photo strips below.

News flash: There is **NOTHING** wrong with being sensitive.

Do your feelings get hurt easily? Do you start feeling sad when someone is being mean? Do you feel overwhelmed by your thoughts?

Being sensitive is not a weakness. It means you care. It gives you the tools to be a better friend.

Being seen with my parents

So many things feel embarrassing when you're growing up.

Here are some things that embarrassed me when I was younger.

Feeling alone at a Party

Things I was embarrassed about

Having frizzy hai[r]

Wearing the wrong clothes

Saying something stupid

What things
embarrass
you?

Draw them here.

If you're feeling sad or lonely and you want to find help but are afraid to ask, you're not alone. It can be really hard to tell someone how you're feeling. It's even harder to talk to someone when you're angry or upset.

PEOPLE WANT TO HELP YOU!

What's On Your Mind?

Fill these bubbles with thoughts that make you feel down. Sharing what's troubling you will help you feel so much better and less alone.

My teacher is mean.

The Healing Power of Touch

Next time you're feeling down, try giving a friend
a hug, petting a dog, or cuddling a cat.
You're sure to feel better in no time!

When people feel overwhelmed, angry, and lonely for a really long time, it might be more than sadness. They may be dealing with depression. Depression may make you feel like you don't want to see anyone. While at the same time, you might feel sooo lonely you could cry.

It's the most bizarre, confusing, lonely feeling in the world. And sometimes you wish someone would look behind your angry exterior and literally fight to hug you.

There's a difference between feeling sad and feeling depressed. Sad feelings can come and go, but depressed feelings can stay for much longer. Write an emotional moment or experience you have had in each circle. Draw sun triangles around depressed feelings, and draw petals around sad feelings.

Want to sleep all the time

Crying for hours and days

Fight with best friend

Just ask!

If you ever feel depressed,
asking for help is
such a brave (and necessary)
thing to do!

Here are some ways to ask for help:

- Talk to your teacher after class.

- Ask your parent to take you to a doctor.

- Visit your school's nurse or counselor.

- Write a note to someone asking for help.

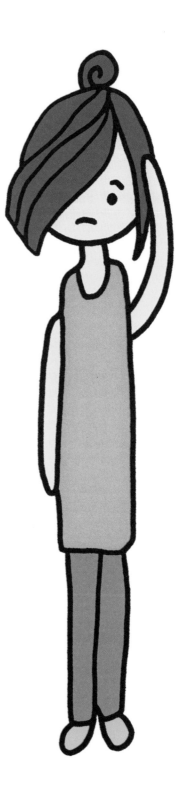

Draw yourself some "Brave Girl" badges because you are a BRAVE girl!

BRAVE GIRLS

TRIED NEW FOOD!
dragon fruit

MADE NEW FRIEND

TRIED TO PLAY NEW SPORT

You are
Amazing!
You are
Brave!
You are
Strong!

Life is full of ups and downs like a weird carnival ride.
Days, weeks, or months might be amazing, then
WHAM—a hard day arrives.

{ BOUNCING BACK }

Bouncing back gets easier.
Your inner strength is like a muscle. Each time you pull
yourself back up, your resilience muscle gets stronger.

UP
AND

D
O
W
N

a
r
e
My

EMOTIONS

Do you have any friends who seem like they're struggling? Try doing something fun together like coloring, painting your nails, or watching a movie. What activities would you do with your friend for Cheer-Up Day?

Operation Cheer-Up Day!

10 a.m.: _____   2 p.m.: _____

11 a.m.: _____   3 p.m.: _____

12 p.m.: _____   4 p.m.: _____

1 p.m.: _____   5 p.m.: _____

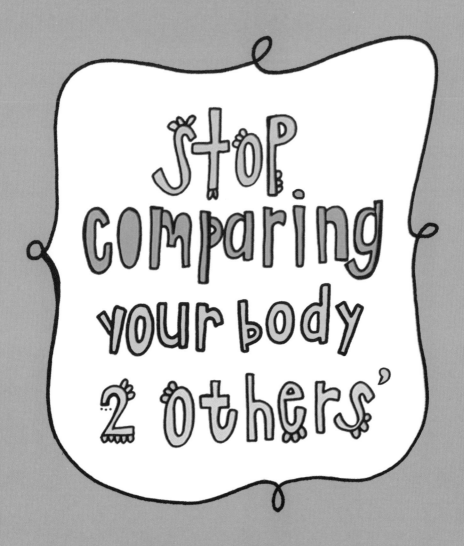

Chapter Four

STOP comparing your body 2 others'

You are perfect just the way you are.

True Beauty

No, seriously! Being you, "flaws" and all—that's true beauty!

TV, magazines, and even your friends and family might try to convince you that you're better off looking like someone else.

Don't listen!

Just remember you are YOU—and that's pretty awesome.

Have you ever disliked a part of your body?
(I know I have!)

Almost everyone dislikes something about their physical appearance. But why do we feel like we aren't enough?

We shouldn't have to change ourselves to feel beautiful.

Beauty is about SO much more than just our appearance—it's about our spirit!

Remember, there has never been someone exactly like you—that is why you are beautiful!

It's easy to dislike certain parts of your body, but make sure you don't forget about the parts you love!

For instance, I love my eyelashes!

List the body parts you love below.

-
-
-
-
-
-

YOUR BODY (is) Wonderful, just the way it is!

YAY!

HOPE

Wouldn't it be incredible if we all embraced our differences?

Short, tall, big, small—be proud of who you are.
It's easy to get discouraged when you don't fit a certain
mold, but it's important to remember to appreciate
the differences in yourself and others.

EMBRACE CHANGE

We all grow at different times and speeds.

Some of us are excited for the change, but for some of us it is super annoying. It definitely was for me. My hair was always frizzy, and my pimples were in competition with my freckles to see which could make more spots first!

Everyone's body changes a bunch of times throughout their lives.

Yours will, too, and that's okay!

It can be strange when your classmates come back after summer break looking so different. It's especially weird when you feel like you haven't changed at all. Be patient—your body has its own pace that's exactly right for you.

Draw your self-portrait from the first day of kindergarten to the future you.

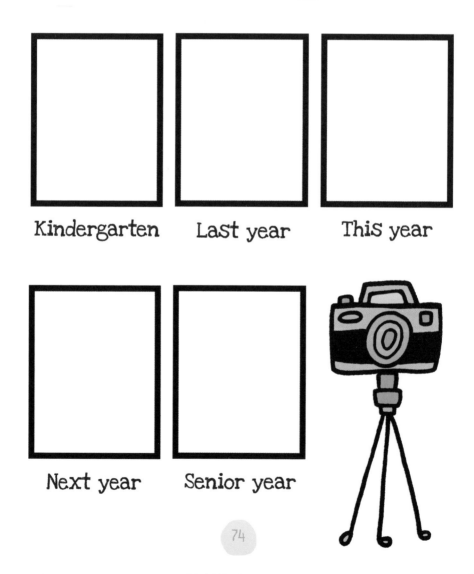

Kindergarten   Last year   This year

Next year   Senior year

We may all look different on the outside.

But on the inside, we're quite similar.

It's easy to become a little obsessed with your appearance or weight. You may even be tempted to try to change your body in unsafe ways. It can be hard to turn off the negative thoughts in your head.

Fill in some of the worries you think about.

Not eating enough can make you sick, causing:

*Weakness
*Headaches
*Hair loss
*Sore bones

If you or someone you know is eating too little,
please talk to an adult you trust for help.
Create your own healthy after-school snack.

Recipe: AFteR-ScHooL ≥SnacK≥

Directions:

_____
_____
_____
_____
_____

INgredients:

_____
_____
_____
_____

i Refuse to Feel ashamed of my BODY.

You can't always know what your friends are struggling with on the inside. So try to avoid making comments— good or bad!—about a person's weight or appearance.

Look Behind the Masks

I am so tall, I feel like a giraffe.

I am so small, I feel like a little kid.

I feel like a whale.

Draw the mask you hide behind.

April 13
Dear Diary,

Someone told me I looked "sickly" today . . .
like too skinny.

I didn't know there was such a thing as
TOO THIN. All the magazines and TV shows
have super-skinny people and everyone tells
them how pretty they are.

It's so confusing!

Today I realized maybe I am too skinny. I got
scared and asked to go to a doctor to help
me become a healthy weight again.

Love, Jen

Be your own kind of beautiful.

Draw a portrait of yourself embracing
all the "flaws" that make you special.
Remember, there is no "normal."

Chapter Five

BE YOURSELF, always

Unique quirks and all!

THE WORLD NEEDS YOU TO BE YOU.

If someone is being mean to others, they're acting like a bully. No one likes to be pushed around or teased.

Be a leader instead of a bully. Help bring people together and protect them from trouble, and use your voice to make good ideas heard.

You can use humor and funny jokes to make everyone laugh together instead of laughing at one person.

What is your favorite joke? Write it here:

_____

Everyone has their own unique personality, and that's a great thing! Some traits can help you be the BEST version of yourself. Here are some positive personality traits.

Confidence

You believe in yourself and trust what you're doing.
You speak up and make yourself heard.

Bravery

You push yourself to try new things and grow
your skills, even if it's scary.

Patience

You take the necessary time to figure something out.
You don't give up easily.

Forgiveness

You let things go and give others a second chance—and you
realize everyone makes mistakes, even you!

Grade yourself on all the (A+mazing) personality traits that represent you!

Report card

Confidence ☐

Bravery ☐

Patience ☐

Forgiveness ☐

Add your own ☐

Circle the positive words that describe you now in one color, and cross out the words you hope to be in another color.

Confident

Courageous

Thoughtful

Colorful

KIND

Clever

Peaceful

Loving

Patient

Affectionate

Calm

Smart

Honest

Generous

BRAVE

Forgiving

Humble

Hopeful

Focused

Healthy

Organized

Sincere

Polite

Funny

Friendly

Bold

Mature

Gentle

Creative

Fair

Flexible

Circle the negative words that describe you now
in one color, and cross out the words you
hope to overcome in another color.

Strange

Thin-skinned

Possessive

Lazy

Strict

Impatient

LOUD

Lonely

Quick-tempered

Jealous

Selfish

Picky

Irresponsible

Tardy

Feisty

Insecure

Distracted

Gullible

Stubborn

Spoiled

Harsh

Egotistical

Cynical

Sarcastic

Nosy

BORED

Shy

Depressed

Fearful

Cold

Pessimistic

Messy

Moody

Mean

Clingy

You were born to be real, not perfect.

We want everything to be perfect in our lives, but sometimes that isn't possible. People make mistakes, and things don't always go as planned. But unexpected twists can turn into something even better!

Draw a flower next to the one below. Then draw a second one next to it but change one thing.

Now look at it with a fresh perspective.

The flower I drew is FAR from perfect, and the one you drew is probably just as imperfect. But the imperfections make them interesting and unique!

Just like there are positive personality traits,
there are negative ones, too.

While it may be hard to stay calm during stressful
situations, being disrespectful, unfriendly, angry,
or argumentative won't help.

Try your best to breathe and keep your cool
even if you disagree.

Be kind to others, especially those
who may have different views than you.

They might become friends who will teach
you something new and help you grow!

Be kind to one another.

Celebrate the quirky things about yourself by drawing comics about them. These are the things that make you special!

Here are some of my weird comics.

Draw your own weird comics.

Design a dream bedroom that perfectly captures your personality!

Quiz: Are you right-brained or left-brained?

1. Someone gave you a brand-new remote-control car. You . . .

a. read the directions before using it.

b. jump right in and give it a test-drive.

2. You just got an assignment to research your family tree. You . . .

a. think the whole project through before working on it.

b. spontaneously work on bits and pieces before hitting the books.

3. When a problem strikes, you . . .

a. use facts to solve it.

b. use your gut to solve it.

4. You just got new posters to hang on your wall. You . . .

a. measure the wall and the poster to make sure everything's even.

b. hang them up wherever you think they look good.

5. In school, you are more drawn to . . .

a. science and math.

b. art and music.

Key:

If you answered mostly *a*, you are . . . left-brained!

If you answered mostly *b*, you are . . . right-brained!

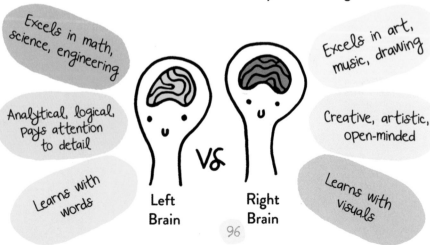

Excels in math, science, engineering

Analytical, logical, pays attention to detail

Learns with words

Excels in art, music, drawing

Creative, artistic, open-minded

Learns with visuals

Left Brain

VS

Right Brain

{ draw or write }

What Makes You Awesome

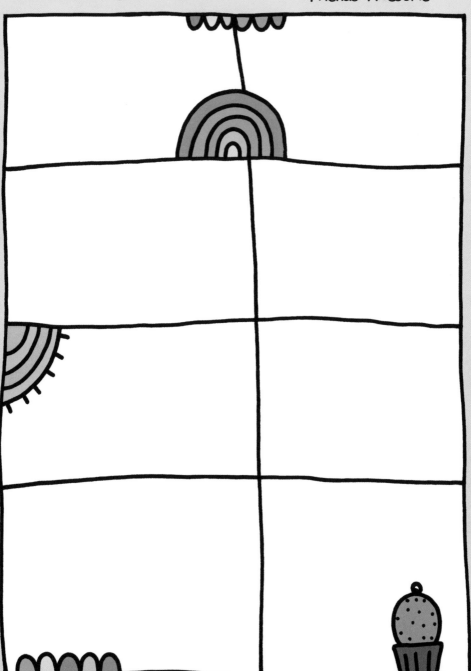

Chapter Six

BE Grateful

Giving thanks just once each day will make life {feel} BETTER!

Try to find things you're grateful for even on your worst days. It's hard sometimes! But being thankful reminds us that the world is full of gifts and wonders.

Write the things you're grateful for until this page is full. Then keep the good feelings going by starting a gratitude notebook!

KEEP YOUR EYES OPEN!

little gifts of happiness are Everywhere.

5 ways to become more GRATEFUL

1. Look for an unexpected "gift of the day" to celebrate a small moment of joy.

2. Think of the best things that happened each day before you fall asleep.

3. Say "thank you" more often.

4. Do something nice for someone without being asked.

5. Let the amazing people around you know that you appreciate them.

Thankful Family Tree

Use the leaves to write down who you are most thankful for. Even if someone is not related to you, they can still be a part of your thankful family.

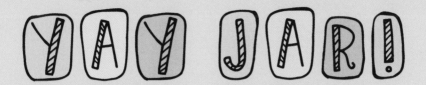

YAY JAR!

Write a happy moment or proud achievement on each slip of paper in the Yay Jar below. You may want to create a real Yay Jar for yourself. Sometimes it helps to read the wonderful memories when you're feeling down or having a bad day.

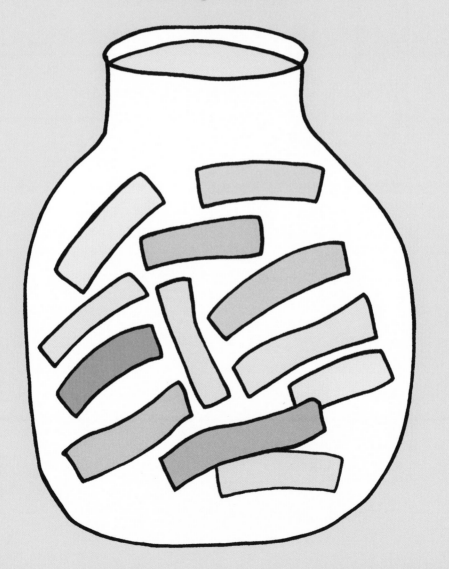

Write thank-you notes to important people in your life.

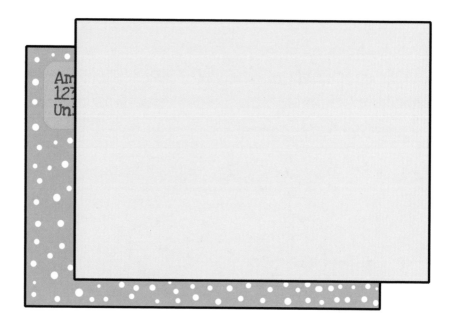

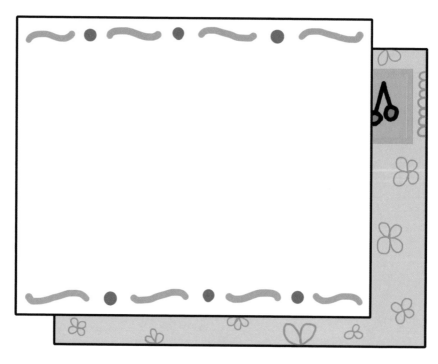

Design your own stamps to "mail" the notes.

Chapter Seven

DREAM BIG

Following your heart's passions will make life GRAND!

We are all very different from one another, so it only makes sense for our goals and dreams to be different, too.

Throughout your life you will try many activities and have lots of little dreams. Some will stick and some will come and go, but they will all lead you closer to finding your big dreams.

everyone has BIG dreams
(small ones, too).
YOU just have to work hard to reach them!

Write your big and small dreams in the clouds below.

Hobbies can keep you happy when life gets hard. They also can lead you toward your dreams. So whether you love dogs, plants, cooking, writing, magic, politics, painting, inventing, personal fitness, or anything else— dream, dream, DREAM!

★ Do things that excite you.

Don't worry if other people don't think your passion matters or is cool.

change the world

cook

garden

create you

MOOD

Cut out (or draw) images that inspire you—anything from empowering words to photos from magazines. Make a collage!

own...

BOARD

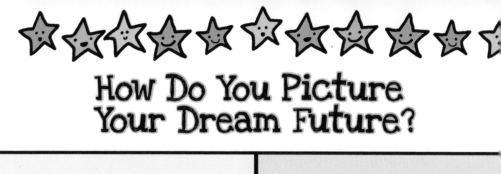

How Do You Picture Your Dream Future?

Your ideal family	Your dream job
Your dream home	Your dream hobby

Goal List

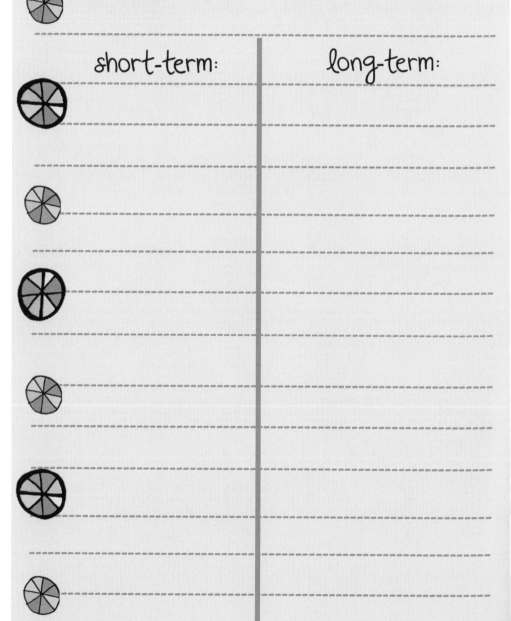

short-term:

long-term:

DON'T GIVE UP!

It's important to know that sometimes you will try and fail. And that's okay! Many famous people did not succeed on their first try.

Here are just a few:

Walt Disney

Albert Einstein

Oprah Winfrey

J. K. Rowling

Steven Spielberg

Lady Gaga

Steve Jobs

Vincent van Gogh

Theodor Seuss Geisel
aka Dr. Seuss

Marilyn Monroe

Jay-Z

Michael Jordan

Dreams take work!

Write your dream in the cloud below
and list the steps you will take
to help achieve your dream.

Draw an encouraging poster to keep yourself motivated.

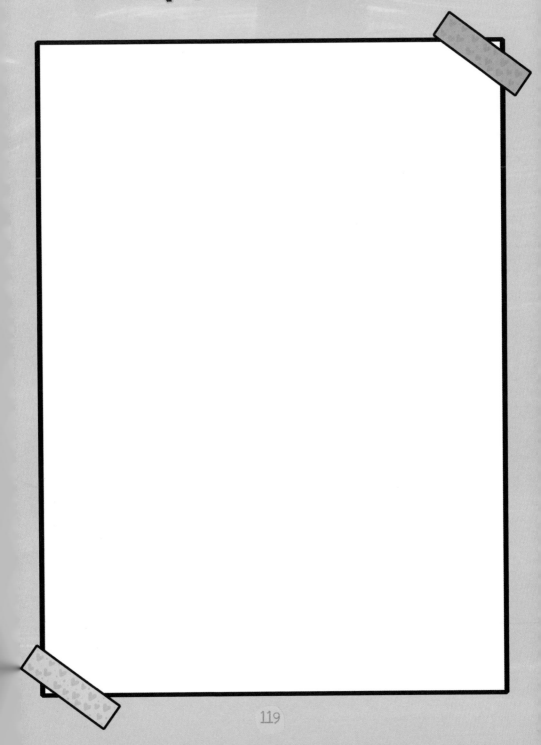

Congratulations!

· · · · · · · · · · ·

You achieved your goal of . . .

_____

_____

_____

_____
date

· · · · · · · · · · ·

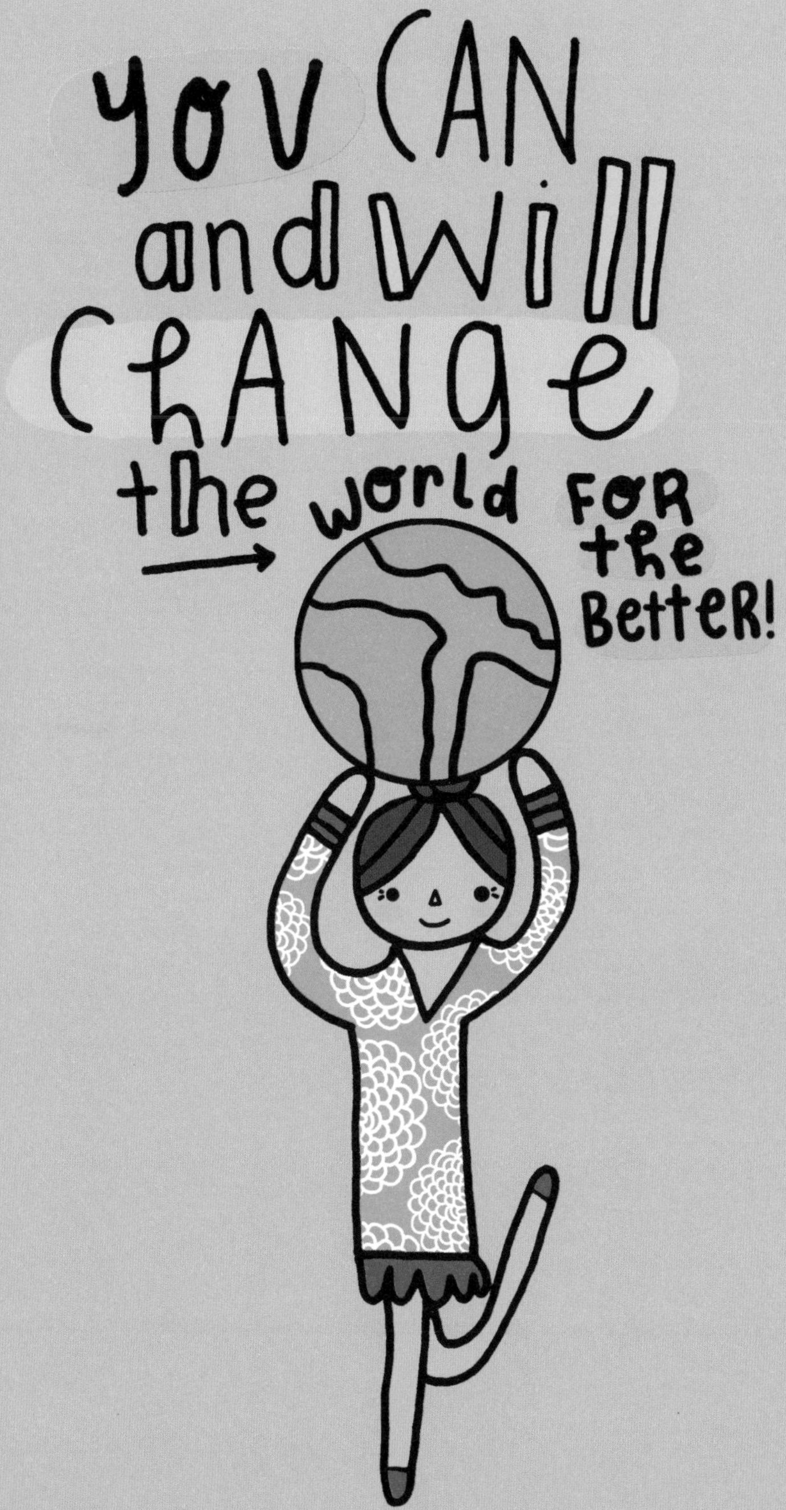
YOU CAN and Will CHANGE the world FOR the BETTER!

DRAW A self-portrait

when you finish this book.

Write a letter to your future self.

It takes sunshine
and rain to
make a rainbow.

Acknowledgments

Good golly, I am so excited you're reading this book! I hope it helps you follow your dreams and realize how completely awesome you are! ♥

Camilo, thanks for keeping me sane, showing me cute animal videos, and giving me oodles of hugs. You are my favorite person in the universe, and this book couldn't have happened without your support. ☺

To Amanda G., Queenie B., Lara H., Yolli S. + Brandy W.— thank you for being there while I wrote, sketched, drew, inked, and colored these pages. Thanks for encouraging texts and cookie breaks. I couldn't have done it without you! ♥

To my agent Ashley, my editors Sam, Emily, and Maria, and all the wonderful people at Crown and Penguin Random House—thank you for giving me the opportunity to share this book with the world!

And thanks to all my internet friends, acquaintances, and cheerleaders for inspiring me to keep following my dreams, even on the hard days! ♥

About the Author

Jenipher Lyn is a professional artist whose clients include Design House Greetings, Women You Should Know, St. Jude Children's Research Hospital, and Girls on the Run. Her paper products have been featured in twenty-two stores, including Target and Trader Joe's. You can follow her on Facebook at NightlyDoodles and on Instagram at @jenipherlyn, or visit her at JenipherLyn.com.

Dedication

Camilo, thanks for loving me just the way
I am—flaws and all. I am forever grateful for you. ♥
And to Ollie—following your dreams may not
always be easy, but it is ALWAYS worth it. ♥